DELTA BLUE

HALLOWED GROUND

Russell Robison

Llumina Press

Copyright © 2005 Russell Robison

All rights reserved. No part of this publication may be reproduced or transmitted in any form or by any means electronic or mechanical, including photocopy, recording, or any information storage and retrieval system, without permission in writing from both the copyright owner and the publisher.

Requests for permission to make copies of any part of this work should be mailed to Permissions Department, Llumina Press, PO Box 772246, Coral Springs, FL 33077-2246

Library of Congress Control Number: 2005902943

ISBN: PB 1-59526-071-4

Printed in the United States of America by Llumina Press

DEDICATION

THIS BOOK IS DEDICATED TO ALL OF THE MEN AND WOMEN OF THE UNITED STATES ARMED FORCES WHO HAVE SERVED, AND ARE SERVING OUR COUNTRY. AS ALWAYS, WITH A SPECIAL THANKS TO THE MOBILE RIVERINE FORCE, TF116,TF117,THE 9TH INFANTRY DIVISION, YRBM-17, AND NSA-DONG TAM.

BUT ESPECIALLY FOR

LT. JAMES B. ROBISON USN.
U.S.S. SAGE AM111
PACIFIC THEATRE
1942-1945

THANKS DAD

FOREWORD

I walked among giants, and they called me brother……….

RUSSELL G. ROBISON GMG-3
UNITED STATES NAVY
NSA-DONG TAM RVN
FEB 68 – MAY 70

May we always remember those who sacrificed their tomorrows so that we might have today

DELTA BLUE

TABLE OF CONTENTS

HALLOWED GROUND	1
MAKE A STAND	2
THEIR STORY	3
AND SO IT GOES	4
WE WALKED AWAY	5
WHEN LOVE IS THERE	6
THE FIGHT	7
911	8
LETTERS FROM THE DARK FILE	9
BAD TIMING	10
JUST PASSING THROUGH	11
OLD MAN RIVER	12
THE CORPSMAN	13
DOUBTS	14
GUILT	15
THE RAIN	16
JUST A THOUGHT #3	17
RAGE	18
QUESTIONS	20
STUFF	21
SOUL SURRENDER	23
THE RIVER	24
THEY TELL ME	25
NOWHERE MAN	27
MINDLESS	28
FIRE	29
SONG	30
LAUGHING EYES	31
GOING SOMEWHERE	32
HOMELAND	33
NO MATTER NOW	34
THINKING OUT LOUD	35
HATE	36
GO FIGURE	37

PLACES	38
KINDRED	39
BEHAVIORS	40
BOOKENDS	41
COMING DOWN HARD	42
POLITICIANS	44
THE CHILDREN	45
BOOT CAMP SONG	46
CHILLICOTHE, TEXAS	48
INDIFFERENCE	50
PRIVELDGE	51
THE DOCTOR	52
THE WOOD CARVER	53
THE LIGHT	54
JINGLE BELLS	55
JOESEPHINE	57
WHISPERS ON THE WIND	58
LOVE	59
MY LADY	60
HOT RAILS TO HELL	62
THE WALK	64
BULLDOZER	65
TRUCKIN	66
SOLUTIONS	67
PLACES	68
MY CAR	69
NAMES	70
GUITAR MAN	71
DIATRIBE	72
SIILY STUFF	73
THE FECAL MATTER	75
HOW SWEET THE LIGHT	76
BREAK THE CHAIN	77
THE LAST MISSION	78
REQUIEM	80
FARE THEE WELL	82
PENANCE	83

HALLOWED GROUND

MUCH TOO DEARLY,
MUCH TOO DEEP.
THIS GROUND SO SACRED
IN OUR KEEP.

PURCHASED
IN THE HARSHEST WAY,
THAT HUMAN BEINGS
EVER PAY.

DISTANT CONFLICTS,
FOREIGN LAND,
DEFENDED
WITH THE BLOOD OF MAN.

SIGNAL HONOR;
GREAT THE COST.
GUARANTEED
WITH FUTURES LOST.

THE LONELY TRUMPET,
THE SADDEST SOUND,
FOREVER HEARD
ON HALLOWED GROUND.

DELTA BLUE

MAKE A STAND

WORDS I DID NOT WANT TO HEAR
NOW ECHOED LOUDLY IN MY EAR.
AMBUSHED IN A FOREIGN LAND,
THERE CAME THE CALL TO MAKE A STAND.

NO WARNING GIVEN, WE DID LEARN
THAT FIRE CAN TEACH YOU AS YOU BURN.
A SHATTERED SILENCE, FEAR DID REIGN,
I NEVER KNEW THERE WAS SUCH PAIN.

AND YES, IT STILL AMAZES ME
HOW TWISTED TIMES REALITY.
WHAT SEEMED LIKE HOURS, SECONDS SPENT,
THE GUNS FELL SILENT, HEAVEN SENT.

SOMETIMES YOU HAVE TO STAND YOUR GROUND,
NO MATTER HOW IT'S GOING DOWN.
WE GRABBED OUR SOULS AND HELD ON TIGHT,
'CAUSE HADES CAME TO PLAY THAT NIGHT.

DELTA BLUE

THEIR STORY

OH, DID I TELL THEIR STORY?
OH, DID I TELL IT TRUE?
CAN YOU UNDERSTAND MY FRIEND,
WHAT I'M TRYING TO SAY TO YOU?

NO, IT WAS NOT FOR GLORY,
NO, IT WAS NOT FOR FAME.
NO, IT WAS NOT FOR MONEY,
NO, IT WAS NOT A GAME.

THEY DID IT FOR THEIR COUNTRY,
AND A CAUSE THEY THOUGHT WAS TRUE.
THEY DIDN'T DO IT FOR THEMSELVES,
THEY DID IT ALL FOR YOU.

THEY ASKED FOR NOTHING IN RETURN,
FOR THE SACRIFICES MADE.
SO NEVER IN YOUR HEART FORGET,
THE PRICE THAT THEY ALL PAID.

DELTA BLUE

AND SO IT GOES

IT'S ALWAYS IN THEIR EYES, THAT GAZE.
A MARKER OF TOO MANY DAYS.
SO HAUNTING, DISTANT, FAR AWAY,
YOU CAN'T MISTAKE THAT LOOK THEY SAY.

IT'S IN THEIR EYES THE STORIES TOLD,
AND IN THE SOUL WHERE BLOOD RUNS COLD.
YES, IT'S THE EYES THAT ALWAYS TELL,
OF TOO MUCH TIME SPENT LIVING HELL.

YOU STAND THE LINE, YOU TAKE THE BLOW
AND NOT A TEAR CAN EVER SHOW.
YOU ARE THE ROCK, YOU CANNOT FLEE,
YOUR PUNISHMENT IS THAT YOU SEE.

AND AS THE SEARING SCAR IS MADE.
FOREVER MORE THE SHADOWS FADE.
IT WAS A TIME OF PAINFUL LIGHT,
THAT GAVE THEM ALL TOO MUCH OF SIGHT.

I SING A SONG OF MAN'S LAMENT.
FOR ALL THE SACRIFICES SPENT.
AND HAVE THE CHOIR RECALL A HYMN,
FOR THOSE WHOSE SIGHT IS STILL SO GRIM.

AND SO THE ENDLESS STORY GOES.
FOR EVERMORE THE HARSHEST BLOWS.
AS CANYONS ECHO TO THE SOUND,
THAT TERROR MAKES WHEN DEATH IS FOUND.

AND THOUGH THE CONFLICTS NEVER CEASE,
SEEMS THERE'S NO PROFIT FOUND IN PEACE.
TOO MANY NEVER RECOGNIZE,
THE TRUTH THAT BURNS INSIDE THEIR EYES.

DELTA BLUE

WE WALKED AWAY

WE LOOKED THEM IN THE EYE THAT DAY,
WE GAVE OUR WORD, WE SAID WE'D STAY.
THAT SIDE BY SIDE WE'D HELP THEIR DREAM,
THOUGH WAR'S AN ANSWER SO EXTREME.

AND SO WE JOINED THEM IN THE FIGHT,
WE DID OUR BEST TO MAKE THINGS RIGHT.
BUT WAY BACK HOME THE HEART BEAT COLD,
'TWAS NOT A TIME FOR BEING BOLD.

SO WE BECAME A NIGHTMARE'S DAWN,
A TWISTED POLITICIAN'S SPAWN.
WHERE NO ONE HAD THE HEART TO RULE,
SO WE BECAME A USELESS TOOL.

NOW VICTORY IS NEVER FOUND,
WHEN INDECISION RULES THE GROUND.
THERE WAS NO HONOR, SAVE FOR THOSE
WHO FOUGHT AND DIED, AND SO IT GOES.

SO LIONS FELL WHILE COWARDS SPIT.
THE TORCH HAD FALLEN, NEVER LIT.
WE LOST OUR WILL, AND THEN OUR WAY,
TO THOSE WHO FELL WHAT DO WE SAY?

WHEN LEADERSHIP HAS LOST ITS SIGHT,
YOU DON'T ABANDON THOSE WHO FIGHT.
I STILL CAN HEAR MY FATHER SAY,
"DON'T GIVE YOUR WORD, AND WALK AWAY."

DELTA BLUE

WHEN LOVE IS THERE

THE LIFELESS SMILE,
THE SPIRIT COLD,
WHERE ONCE HAD BURNED,
A FIRE SO BOLD.

THE BATTERED HEART,
THE TROUBLED EYES,
TOO LITTLE TRUTH,
TOO MANY LIES.

THE DOWNWARD GAZE,
THE MUFFLED SIGH,
THAT COMES WITH WATCHING
LIFE PASS BY.

THE ACHING NEED,
SO HARD TO BEAR,
HEALED ONLY NOW,
WHEN LOVE IS THERE.

DELTA BLUE

THE FIGHT

HAVE YOU EVER SEEN A FRIEND DIE SLOW?
SO TERRIFIED, BECAUSE THEY KNOW,
THAT DEATH IS NEAR AND SPEAKS THEIR NAME,
WHILE THEY CRY OUT IN FEAR AND PAIN.

AND ALL THERE IS THAT YOU CAN DO,
IS HOLD THEM CLOSE AND TELL THEM TRUE.
TO HOLD ON NOW, THAT YOU ARE THERE,
EASY BROTHER, DON'T DESPAIR.

FOR THOSE OF YOU WHO'VE NEVER KNOWN,
THE PRICES PAID WHEN WAR IS SOWN.
MAY YOUR EYES NEVER SEE THE SIGHT,
OF WHAT TAKES PLACE THERE IN THE FIGHT.

THEY SAY THAT WE WILL NEVER LEARN.
THAT'S WHY AGAIN TO WAR WE TURN.
AND IN OUR FOLLY, AND OUR STRIFE,
WE THROW AWAY TOO MUCH OF LIFE.

THE QUESTIONS MANY, ANSWERS FEW.
SOMETIMES YOU DON'T KNOW WHAT TO DO.
I CANNOT CHANGE WITH ALL MY MIGHT,
THE CONSEQUENCES OF THE FIGHT.

DELTA BLUE

911

IT WAS DONE NOW IN GOD'S NAME
AN ACT THAT ALL COULD SEE INSANE
A NECESSARY DEED THEY CLAIMED
OUR DEATH THEIR GOD HAD NOW ORDAINED

THEY ARE SO WRONG NOW THIS WE KNOW
AND THEY WILL REAP JUST WHAT THEY SOW
AS DEATH IS ALL THEY UNDERSTAND
IT NOW RETURNS TO BURN THEIR LAND

I CLOSE MY FIST AND TURN THEIR WAY
I NEVER WILL FORGIVE THAT DAY
AND IN THIS ACT THEY HOLD SO DEAR
THEY DID NOT FILL OUR HEARTS WITH FEAR

THEY CANNOT CONQUER US WITH HATE
THEIR EMPTY SOULS WILL BE THEIR FATE
YOU STIR A GIANT, FOOLISH YOU
I'LL SAY IT PLAIN: RED, WHITE, AND BLUE

DELTA BLUE

LETTERS FROM THE DARK FILE

WE FOUGHT OUR WAY BACK TO THEM,
THAT BLOODY PLACE STILL MOURNED.
DID ALL WE COULD, JUST AS WE SHOULD,
GAVE SHELTER FROM THE STORM.

STILL WE WERE INSUFFICIENT,
IN OUR COURAGE, AND OUR AIM.
TO PREVENT THE BLOODY SLAUGHTER,
OF THE DYING, AND THE MAIMED.

OH, DARK DISTRUCTIVE CHAOS,
WHERE WE ALL LOST A FRIEND.
PERHAPS THE GREATEST SIN OF ALL
IS THAT IT NEVER ENDS.

INSANITY PERSONIFIED,
BEYOND OUR VISION'S SIGHT.
THIS ANGRY TALE THAT I DETAIL,
OF MADNESS IN THE NIGHT.

AN ENDLESS RETRIBUTION,
A CIRCUMSTANCE OF SHAME.
DECISIONS MADE WHILE WE WERE SLAYED,
IN THE POLITICIAN'S GAME.

DELTA BLUE

BAD TIMING

IT TOOK NO COURAGE, I MUST SAY
WHEN SHRAPNEL JOINED WITH ME THAT DAY.
JUST REAL BAD TIMING, YES INDEED,
AS I SAT AND WATCHED ME BLEED.

MOVE IT MAN, NOW YOU'RE ALL RIGHT.
IT'S JUST A SCRATCH, YOU STILL CAN FIGHT.
A QUICK EXAM FOUND ALL IN PLACE.
I GOT RIGHT BACK INTO THE RACE.

NO FASTER RUNNER HAVE YOU SEEN.
ONE TWENTY -TWO'S ARE JUST PLAIN MEAN.
A SCAR I WEAR NOW FROM THE PAST.
TURNS OUT I WASN'T QUITE THAT FAST.

A MINOR WOUND NOW WAS THE VIEW,
AND SCARED TO DEATH WAS YOU KNOW WHO.
YES, JUST BAD TIMING LONG AGO,
IN THAT DANCE TOO MANY KNOW.

DELTA BLUE

JUST PASSING THROUGH

THEY SAID IT WAS IMPROPER
TO FART IN CHURCH THAT DAY.
I SAID THAT I MEANT NO OFFENSE;
IT JUST CAME OUT THAT WAY.

YOU KNOW GOD UNDERSTANDS IT.
IT'S HIS DESIGN, YOU SEE.
AND I WAS PROPERLY REPENTENT,
AND PROMPTLY TOOK A KNEE.

BUT AS I KNELT TO PRAY THERE,
MY TRUMPET SPOKE ONCE MORE.
AND I HEARD THE SOUND OF PEOPLE
QUICKLY MOVING FOR THE DOOR.

THE MINISTER WAS GAGGING,
THE ORGANIST AGHAST,
AND I DID NOT HAVE THE HEART TO SAY,
"MY FRIENDS, ANOTHER'S PASSED."

THE CHOIR'S RETREAT BECAME A ROUT,
THE CONGREGATION FLED.
SAID, "SORRY LORD, JUST PASSING THROUGH."
"I UNDERSTAND," HE SAID.

DELTA BLUE

OLD MAN RIVER

CAST THE LINES OFF, AMMO STOWED;
THE RIVERS CALLING, I AM TOLD.
WEAPONS READY, ALL ON BOARD;
A PRAYER IS OFFERED TO OUR LORD.

KEEP YOUR FOCUS, SHARP THE EYE;
HOLD YOUR FEAR, FOR GOD IS NIGH.
LOCK AND LOAD NOW, HATE THAT SOUND;
IT SAYS WE SAIL FOR ANGRY GROUND.

THE FADING SUN, NOW TAKES THE LIGHT;
WE TURN OUR BOW INTO THE NIGHT.
THE RUMBLING DIESEL'S TALK TO ME;
OLD MAN RIVER, LEAVE US BE.

DELTA BLUE

THE CORPSMAN

"I'M HIT, I'M HIT," NOW CAME THE CRY.
THE CORPSMAN DID NOT QUESTION WHY.
HE CRAWLED OUT TO THE FALLEN MAN,
TO HEAL HIS WOUNDS, THAT WAS HIS PLAN.

AMIDST THE MADNESS ALL AROUND,
THE CORPSMAN DID NOT HEAR A SOUND.
AS TRACERS RIPPED ACROSS THE NIGHT;
HE WOULD NOT GIVE UP ON THIS FIGHT.

"HANG ON MAN, FOR I AM HERE"
"YOU HAVE NO REASON NOW TO FEAR."
HE'D SEEN TOO MANY DIE, AND SO
HIS HANDS MOVED QUICKLY, IN THE KNOW.

BUT AS HE SAW HIM SLIP AWAY,
HE CURSED THE PRICE THIS MAN DID PAY.
ANOTHER BROTHER, TORN APART,
HAD BROKEN ONCE MORE, THIS CORPSMAN'S HEART.

DELTA BLUE- THE MADNESS

DOUBTS

SHOULD I LET THIS DEMON LAY?
THAT LIVES INSIDE THE WORDS I SAY.
HAVE I SAID TOO MUCH, TOO LONG?
DO I DISRESPECT THEIR SONG?

SHOULD I NOT TELL OF THE FIGHT?
AND TALK ABOUT WHAT THEY DID RIGHT.
THAT QUESTION ALWAYS PULLS AT ME,
SHOULD I BE STILL AND LET IT BE?

NOW SAY NO MORE OF ALL THEY'VE DONE,
THROUGH SACRIFICE AND HONOR WON.
SO MANY WORDS, SO MANY YEARS,
DID I SPEAK TOO OFTEN OF THEIR FEARS?

NO MATTER HOW LONG THAT I WRITE,
THERE ARE NO WORDS TO SAY IT RIGHT.
I STUMBLE DOWN A TWISTED ROAD
JUST TRYING TO LIGHTEN UP THE LOAD.

DELTA BLUE

GUILT

I'M TOLD THE FEELING'S COMMON,
IN THOSE WHO DID SURVIVE.
THIS ACHE THAT I STILL CARRY,
'CAUSE I CAME BACK ALIVE.

NOW I DON'T MAKE EXCUSES,
NOR DO I TELL A LIE.
INSIDE I STILL FEEL GUILTY,
THAT THERE I DID NOT DIE.

THIS FEELING LIVES INSIDE ME,
THIS THING I STILL REGRET.
WHY THEM INSTEAD OF ME NOW?
AND THEM I CAN'T FORGET.

NOW I HAVE BLED IN BATTLE,
THOUGH NEVER DID I FALL.
BY GRACE I WAS EXCLUDED,
FROM THOSE WHO GAVE THEIR ALL.

DELTA BLUE

THE RAIN

THE RAIN IS FALLING DOWN TODAY,
IT'S JUST GOD'S TEARS OR SO THEY SAY.
A PROMISE KEPT TO WASH US CLEAN,
A RAINBOW SENT TO MARK THE SCENE.

IT'S ALWAYS MAGIC ANY DAY,
WHEN THE RAIN HAS HAD ITS SAY.
A VITAL MOMENT, DEARLY SOUGHT,
ONCE MORE THE CYCLE, HEAVEN BROUGHT.

THE FALLING RAIN, A SPECIAL SOUND,
RENEWING NOW THE THIRSTING GROUND.
A GIFT OF LIFE FROM UP ABOVE,
TO NOURISH US, AN ACT OF LOVE.

DELTA BLUE

JUST A THOUGHT # 3

WE ALL LIVE IN A WORLD OF DARKNESS.

WE ALL HAVE LANDS WHERE SHADOWS ROAM.

WE ALL INSTINCTIVELY SEEK OUT THE LIGHT,

FOR OUR EYES MUST SEE.

BUT IS IT NOT SAD THAT WE DON'T REALIZE?

OUR EYES ARE BLIND,

YOU SEE WITH THE HEART.

DELTA BLUE

RAGE

THERE IS A RAGE THAT BURNS IN ME,
SOMETIMES SO BRIGHT I CANNOT SEE,
ACROSS MY DARK AND TROUBLED LAND,
IT RULES NOW WITH AN IRON HAND.

AND AS IT BURNS INSIDE MY HEART;
I FEAR THE FIRE THAT IT CAN START.
THE PRAYER I SPEAK INSIDE MY SOUL,
IS THAT IT NEVER TAKES CONTROL.

MY RAGE IS MINE, AND MINE ALONE.
IT COMES FROM TIMES THAT I HAVE KNOWN.
IT FILLS MY OFTEN TROUBLED MIND
WITH ANGRY THOUGHTS TOO LONG UNKIND.

NOW DEMONS DO NOT EVER FADE,
UNLESS THEY'RE FACED AND FINALLY SLAYED.
IT DOESN'T MATTER IF YOU WIN,
BUT THAT YOU RISE TO FIGHT AGAIN.

THIS RAGE WILL NEVER DIE, I KNOW.
STILL I REFUSE TO LET IT GROW.
YES, IT IS MINE ALONE TO KEEP,
SOMETIMES IT CALLS ME WHEN I SLEEP.

A PART OF ME THAT COST SO DEAR;
A SIDE OF ME I OFTEN FEAR.
FOR I KNOW WHERE THE LIGHT CAN'T GO,
DEEP IN THOSE CANYONS THAT I KNOW.

THERE'S NO SURRENDER, NO RETREAT;
FOR ME IT KNOWS IT CAN'T DEFEAT.
THOUGH VIGILANT I DO REMAIN,
TOO OFTEN NOW IT BRINGS THE PAIN.

IT'S WE WHO CHOOSE WHAT RULES INSIDE,
AND WHETHER HATE OR LOVE ABIDE.
SOMEDAY I KNOW I'LL FIND THAT DOOR
THAT LEADS ME FROM THAT CRAZY WAR.

DELTA BLUE

QUESTIONS

THE ENEMY DECIDED WRONG,
THAT MORNING THEY ATTACKED OUR DAWN.
THEY NEVER HAD A CHANCE, THAT'S TRUE;
ANOTHER DAY IN DELTA BLUE.

IN JOYOUS SILENCE, LIFE RETURNS;
UNANSWERED DOUBT FOREVER BURNS.
SURVIVORS QUESTION, NOW THEIR GRACE,
AS OTHERS FELL TO TAKE THEIR PLACE.

SAD AND SACRED SACRIFICE;
YOU CANNOT COMPREHEND THE PRICE;
BEYOND ALL REASON, WRONG OR RIGHT,
THESE THINGS NOW DONE BEFORE OUR SIGHT.

NOW IN MY HEART I KNOW IT'S TRUE;
THERE MUST BE SOMETHING WE CAN DO.
THIS CHILD HAS SEEN ENOUGH I SAY;
IT'S TIME TO FIND ANOTHER WAY.

MY GOD, I DO NOT UNDERSTAND,
THIS CANNOT BE WHAT YOU HAD PLANNED.
THE ONLY QUESTION TO REMAIN,
IS WHY YOUR TRUTH WE STILL DISDAIN?

DELTA BLUE

STUFF

ONCE I WANDERED FAR FROM HOME,
INTO LANDS WHERE NONE SHOULD ROAM.
COMPELLED BY THOUGHTS STILL PART OF ME;
UNWILLING STILL TO LET ME BE.

THOUGH TIMES REMORSE CAN NEVER CURE
THOSE THINGS NOW DONE THAT STILL ENDURE.
THESE HANDS THAT CHOSE TO TAKE A LIFE,
THIS HEART THAT'S FILLED WITH ONLY STRIFE

SOME SAY I DO NOT BEAR THE BLAME,
FOR ACTIONS TAKEN IN WAR'S FLAME.
BUT IN MY SOUL I SEE IT CLEAR;
YOU DO NOT KILL UNLESS YOU FEAR.

BUT I WAS WEAK AND TRUSTED, SO
SWEPT UP IN THINGS I DID NOT KNOW.
FOR I WAS YOUNG AND STILL A FOOL,
FOR POLITICIANS, JUST A TOOL.

A BRAVE NEW WORLD, OR SO THEY SAID.
THE PRICE WAS CHEAP, UNBURIED DEAD.
ANOTHER LIE, ANOTHER WAR,
SHUT UP AND KILL, THAT'S WHAT YOU'RE FOR.

AT FIRST IT WAS THE PARTY LINE,
THOSE COMMIE PIGS, THOSE FILTHY SWINE.
WE'VE GOT TO STOP THEM HERE AND NOW,
BEFORE THEY TAKE   D. C. SOMEHOW.

"THE DOMINOES WILL FALL," THEY SCREAMED,
BUT THAT TURNED OUT TO BE EXTREME.
AND HISTORY, RECORDS WE ERRED,
TOO BAD SO MANY WERE NOT SPARED.

AND THOUGH THE HONOR STILL WAS MINE,
TO SERVE WITH THOSE WHO STOOD THE LINE.
FOR IT WAS THERE I LOST MY YOUTH,
SURRENDERED TO A THING CALLED TRUTH.

WILL GOD FORGIVE ME NOW FOR THEN?
I TOOK THE LIVES OF SUCH BRAVE MEN.
WHO FOUGHT TO FREE THEIR LAND AND WAY,
AND TRUST ME NOW, WE MADE THEM PAY.

NOW WHO ARE WE TO SAY WHAT'S RIGHT?
JUST BECAUSE WE HAVE SUCH MIGHT.
OUR FEARS AND DOUBT LED US TO WAR,
BUT WE KNEW NOT WHAT IT WAS FOR.

THE POLITICIANS DID NOT CARE,
THEIR CHILDREN NEVER OVER THERE.
THEY KEPT THEM SAFE AND FAR AWAY;
"THE RICH DON'T RISK THEIR OWN," THEY SAY.

THERE IS NO REASON I CAN FIND,
FOR ME TO EVER BE SO BLIND.
CONFLICTED I REMAIN, MY FRIENDS,
PERHAPS THAT HOW THE STORY ENDS.

DELTA BLUE

SOUL SURRENDER

BREATH CAME HARD
AS OUR EYES MET.
WE NEVER SPOKE A WORD, AND YET,
THERE WAS A UNION SO SINCERE,
THAT SWEPT AWAY ALL DOUBT AND FEAR.

A SIMPLE TOUCH OF HANDS CONFESSED,
THAT IN OUR HEARTS WE KNEW THE REST.
AND OUR EMBRACE TOLD ALL THE WORLD,
THAT LOVE AGAIN HAD BEEN UNFURLED.

A SOUL SURRENDER, SILENT SAID
THAT FLARED SO BRIGHTLY DARKNESS FLED.
THAT SACRED PLACE WE GO TO HEAL,
BUT ONLY NOW, WHEN LOVE IS REAL.

DELTA BLUE

THE RIVER

CRISP NIGHT AIR WITH SHADOWED MOON,
VEILED IN WHISPY CLOUD'S COCCOON.
THE WIND BLOWS SOFTLY, WATERS FLOW;
THE RIVER IS ALIVE, YOU KNOW.

TEMPTING WITH HER QUIET CALM,
ADRIFT WITHIN HER SPREADING PALM.
BUT DANGER LURKS INSIDE HER HEART,
BE CAREFUL NOW JUST WHAT YOU START.

IT'S NEVER WISE TO BLOCK HER PATH,
AND FOOLISH TO INCURR HER WRATH.
HER SILENT MISSION DONE IN PEACE;
THE RIVER'S JOURNEY WILL NOT CEASE.

A WITNESS TO OUR FOOLISH WAYS,
WE COME AND GO, SHE ALWAYS STAYS.
A TIMELESS PASSAGE, ENDLESS FLOW,
THE RIVER IS ALIVE YOU KNOW.

DELTA BLUE

THEY TELL ME

THEY TELL ME THERE ARE RIVERS,
WHERE THE WATER STILL RUNS CLEAR.
THEY TELL ME THERE ARE PLACES NOW,
WHERE NO ONE LIVES IN FEAR.

THEY TELL ME NOW THAT EVERYTHING,
IS GOING TO BE ALL RIGHT.
THEY SAY THAT WE'VE COME FAR ENOUGH,
TO NO LONGER FEAR THE NIGHT.

THEY TELL ME THAT THE CHILDREN
WILL ALL BE FED TODAY.
THEY TELL ME THAT THE HATRED NOW
IS GOING TO GO AWAY.

THEY TELL NOW TO TRUST THEM,
THAT IT'S NONE OF MY CONCERN.
THAT THE SITUATION'S WELL IN HAND,
AS THEY FIDDLE WHILE WE BURN.

THEY TELL ME I'M A SKEPTIC,
THAT I AM JUST NAIVE.
FOR I WON'T LET THEIR BANTOR
DISAVOW WHAT I PERCEIVE.

BUT FALLING, FALLING, NEVER FREE,
HELD CAPTIVE BY THIS NIGHT.
WHY IS IT THAT WE CANNOT FIND,
OUR WAY BACK TO THE LIGHT?

I NEVER THOUGHT SUCH DARKNESS
COULD EVER COME OUR WAY.
I NEVER DREAMED SUCH MADNESS
COULD EVER CLOUD OUR DAY.

BUT INSIDE OUT AND UPSIDE DOWN,
THIS WORLD IS OFTEN COLD.
WHEN FAITH AND TRUST ARE TURNED TO DOUBT,
THERE'S LESS IN LIFE, I'M TOLD.

DELTA BLUE

NOWHERE MAN

HE IS LOST AND CAN'T BE FOUND;
SOME SAY THAT HE'S GONE UNDERGROUND.
THAT HE HAS TURNED NOW FROM THIS WORLD,
NO LONGER IS HIS FLAG UNFURLED..

HIS BELLY FULL, NOW SOME WOULD SAY,
HE WANTS THE WORLD TO GO AWAY.
NO LONGER DOES HE WISH TO SEE
THIS WORLD THAT'S LOST ITS SANITY.

HE KNOWS THAT HE WILL TAKE THE FALL,
FOR FINALLY HAVING HIT THAT WALL.
NO MORE NOW DOES HE SEEK THE DAY,
GROWN WEARY OF THE DUES TO PAY.

BUT THAT'S AN ISSUE, HIS ALONE;
SOME SAY HE'S JUST TOO FAR FROM HOME.
YES, HE HAS DRIFTED MANY YEARS,
TOO MANY NIGHTS, TOO MANY TEARS.

NOW ALL OF US MUST WALK THE ROAD,
AND ALL OF US MUST BEAR THE LOAD.
BUT WEARY ARMS AND TROUBLED HEART
STILL TRY TO TEAR HIS SOUL APART.

AND THOUGH HE BATTLES ON EACH DAY,
THERE'S REALLY NOTHING MORE TO SAY.
FOR HE IS WEARY OF THIS FIGHT,
LOST IN THIS WORLD HE CAN'T MAKE RIGHT.

DELTA BLUE

MINDLESS

MY GUN WAS SILENT, KNEES WERE BENT,
THE ANGER IN MY HEART WAS SPENT.
UNLEASHED THIS FURY, FOUND TODAY
HAD COME AND GONE, AND HAD ITS SAY.

BUT WHAT REMAINED AT BATTLE'S END,
NO LONGER COULD I COMPREHEND.
ANOTHER SHADOWED, RAGING SON,
TOO FAR FROM HOME, AND NEAR UNDONE.

THIS VISION IN MY MIND RESIDES,
A WOUND THEY NEVER STERILIZED.
FOR IN THAT MADNESS, I DID FIND
INDEED WE ALL HAD LOST OUR MIND.

AND AS WE TEAR THIS WORLD APART,
IN SEARCH OF PEACE, A BRAND NEW START.
WE LET THE PAIN THIS WORLD CAN GIVE
DICTATE TO US, HOW WE WILL LIVE.

DELTA BLUE

FIRE

(lyric)

TIME, SLIPS AWAY,
AND LOVE RULES THE DAY.
WOMAN, NEED YOU SO;
ONLY IN YOUR ARMS, CAN I LOSE CONTROL.
NEED YOUR LOVE, IN THE MORNING.
NEED YOUR LOVE ALL THE DAY.
WOMAN, WOMAN HEAR WHAT I SAY!
NEED YOUR LOVE, ALL NIGHT LONG,
AND WOMAN, WOMAN, MAKE IT STRONG, MAKE IT
STRONG.

FIRE, IN THE NIGHT;
WOMAN, MAKE IT RIGHT.
HEAL ME, IN YOUR FLAME,
WHEN THE DARKNESS COMES, I CRY OUT YOUR NAME.
NEED YOUR LOVE, IN THE MORNING,
NEED YOUR LOVE ALL THE DAY.
WOMAN, WOMAN HEAR WHAT I SAY!
NEED YOUR LOVE, ALL NIGHT LONG,
AND WOMAN, WOMAN, MAKE IT STRONG, MAKE IT
STRONG.

TOO MANY TIMES I'VE TURNED AGAIN TO FACE THE NIGHT,
WITH ONLY YOUR LOVE, TO MAKE EVERYTHING ALL
RIGHT.
FOR ALL THE DAMAGE DONE THAT I CANNOT SUSTAIN;
IT'S ONLY IN YOUR ARMS WHERE I CAN HEAL THE PAIN.

DELTA BLUE

SONG

THERE WAS LOVE IN THE MORNING;
THERE WAS A FIRE PUT THE SUN TO SHAME.
EVERY TIME MY WOMAN, SHE CALLS MY NAME.
SEE HER SHINING, TELLING ME I'M NOT TO BLAME.

WOMAN,
WOMAN,
HOW I LOVE YOU SO.
NEVER LET ME GO.

BEFORE YOU, THERE WAS DARKNESS,
BEFORE YOU, THERE WAS PAIN.
YOU TOOK AWAY THE MADNESS,
AND MADE ME WHOLE AGAIN.

WITH YOUR LOVE, BLIND LOVE,
LIFTING ME JUST A LITTLE BIT HIGHER.
HIGHER, WOMAN NOW I KNOW;
COME FILL MY HEART, WITH YOUR SWEET DESIRE.
WOMAN, WOMAN, HOW I LOVE YOU SO.
NEVER LET ME GO.

BEFORE YOU, THERE WAS DARKNESS,
BEFORE YOU, THERE WAS PAIN.
YOU TOOK AWAY THE MADNESS,
AND MADE ME WHOLE AGAIN.

DELTA BLUE

LAUGHING EYES

LAUGHING EYES FILLED UP THE NIGHT,
THEN TURNED AND LOOKED AT ME.
THERE IS A JOY BEYOND PROFOUND,
THAT'S FOUND IN THOSE WHO SEE.

A WORDLESS CONVERSATION,
A TRUTH WITHOUT DISGUISE.
BEYOND THE CALL OF PASSION AS
THE HEART SPEAKS THROUGH THE EYES.

A CRY TO ALL THE SENSES,
TO AWAKEN TO THE FLAME,
THAT'S FOUND NOW WHEN A SPIRIT
FINDS ANOTHER JUST THE SAME.

DELTA BLUE

GOING SOMEWHERE

WE COULD HAVE BEEN GIANTS,
BUT CHOSE TO BE SMALL.
IN OUR POMPOUS DELUSIONS,
NOW DON'T THAT BEAT ALL?

'CAUSE WHILE WE ALL THOUGHT
WE WERE GOING SOMEWHERE.
TO SEARCH FOR NEW ANSWERS,
AND LEARN WHAT'S OUT THERE.

STILL THINKING WE'RE TRAVELING,
WHILE WALKING IN PLACE.
WE'RE STILL OUT OF FOCUS,
STILL LAST IN THE RACE.

ENROUTE NOW TO MARS,
WHILE THE HUNGRY JUST STARE.
WE STAND HERE CONVICTED,
STILL GOING NOWHERE.

DELTA BLUE

HOMELAND

SEARCHING FOR MY HOMELAND,
AS EACH MORNING I SET SAIL.
IT MATTERS NOT THE DISTANCE,
OR IF ANGRY SEAS PREVAIL.

DON'T KNOW HOW FAR I'LL TRAVEL,
WHERE THIS ROAD WILL CARRY ME.
ONLY KNOW THAT I MUST JOURNEY
TO THAT PLACE WHERE I'LL BE FREE.

IS IT THERE ON THE HORIZON?
THIS WORLD I'VE NEVER KNOWN.
I'M TOLD IT IS THE PROMISED LAND,
A PLACE WHERE PEACE IS GROWN.

I'LL TAKE NOW MY DEPARTURE,
FROM A WORLD THAT WILL NOT SEE.
IT'S ONLY IN SURRENDER
THAT YOU FIND YOUR VICTORY.

DELTA BLUE

NO MATTER NOW

NO MATTER WHERE I GO THIS DAY;
I WILL IGNORE THE PRICE I PAY.
FOR I KNOW ONE THING THAT IS TRUE,
THAT IS THIS LOVE I HAVE FOR YOU.

NO MATTER NOW THE SCARS WITHIN,
FROM ALL THE PLACES I HAVE BEEN.
FOR I KNOW EVEN AS I FALL,
THAT GREATEST TRUTH, LOVE CONQUERS ALL.

NO MATTER NOW THAT I MUST LEAVE,
THERE IS NO REASON NOW TO GRIEVE.
FOR AS I SLIP AWAY, MY FRIEND;
MY LOVE FOR YOU WILL NEVER END.

NO MATTER NOW I CANNOT SEE,
A WORLD THAT DOES NOT INCLUDE ME.
I STEP ASIDE AND SLIP AWAY,
TO LET ANOTHER HAVE THEIR SAY.

I'LL JOIN WITH SPIRITS GONE BEFORE,
INTO THE LIGHT FOREVERMORE,
AND THOUGH MY TIME WITH YOU WILL CEASE,
THAT IS MY ONLY ROAD TO PEACE.

BUT TIME'S RELENTLESS MARCH DEMANDS
I LEAVE MUCH SOONER THAN I PLANNED.
REGRETS REMAIN I MUST ADMIT,
BUT IN THIS WORLD I JUST DON'T FIT.

DELTA BLUE

THINKING OUT LOUD

I ACQUIESED THEIR MUSINGS,
AS THEY TALKED ABOUT GOD'S PLAN,
BUT PEACE WILL NEVER REIGN HERE,
NOT AS LONG AS THERE IS MAN.

IN A NEVER ENDING CIRCLE,
WE HAVE CHOSEN NOT TO LEARN,
AND SO THE PAIN CONTINUES,
FOR HIS TRUTH TOO MANY SPURN.

IN OUR VANITY, SO PETTY;
WE REFUSE TO FREE THOSE CHAINED,
AND FINALLY LET THE PEOPLE
BECOME WHAT HE ORDAINED.

DELTA BLUE

HATE

THEY GOT CAUGHT UP IN THEIR HATE,
NOT KNOWING THAT IT SEALED THEIR FATE.
NOW SOMETHING CLOSES IN THE MIND,
WHEN HATE IS ALL THAT WE CAN FIND.

AND THERE'S NO REASON TO BE FOUND,
WHEN HATE IS ALL THERE IS AROUND.
FOR THEM A MINDLESS STATE OF JOY,
BECAUSE THEIR MINDS, THEY DON'T EMPLOY.

NOW HATRED IS A WASTE OF TIME,
JUST ONE OF MANY OF IT'S CRIMES.
A LEARNED RESPONSE THAT WE ARE TAUGHT,
TO KEEP US FROM THE TRUTH WE SOUGHT.

FOR HATE DIVIDES AND KEEPS US WEAK,
WHEN UNITY IS ALL WE SEEK.
FORGIVE AND HEAL, THAT'S FROM ABOVE;
THE ANSWERS STILL THE SAME, JUST LOVE.

DELTA BLUE

GO FIGURE

AS I LOOK BACK AT MY LIFE NOW,
AND SEE A TRAIL OF DUST.
SEEMS ALL THE DREAMS I'VE EVER HAD,
TURNED OUT TO BE A BUST.

FOREVER QUESTIONS LINGER
INSIDE MY MUDDLED HEAD.
BUT THE ANSWERS STILL ELUDE ME;
I'M JUST CONFUSED, IT'S SAID.

PERHAPS I REACHED MUCH FARTHER
THAN MY ARMS COULD EVER SPAN.
I FIGURE IT WAS NEVER MEANT
TO COME OUT LIKE I PLANNED.

I THOUGHT I'D BE MUCH STRONGER,
AS EACH DAY I FACED THE STORM.
THAT THE TROUBLED SEAS AROUND ME
WOULD NOT REMAIN THE NORM.

I HOPED I'D MAKE A DIFFERENCE;
I THOUGHT I HAD A PLAN.
BUT THAT'S WHAT I GET FOR THINKING,
WHEN I DID NOT UNDERSTAND.

THE GREAT TRUTHS SOME WILL TELL YOU,
ARE PURCHASED AT GREAT COST.
BUT TOO MANY DON'T REMEMBER
WHAT'S BEEN GAINED, AND WHAT'S BEEN LOST.

DELTA BLUE

PLACES

I GUARD A PLACE THAT LIVES IN ME,
WHERE I CAN GO AND YOU CAN'T SEE.
THOSE TIMES WHEN I CAN'T CARRY ON,
THOSE TIMES WHEN I'M NO LONGER STRONG.

A PLACE INSIDE WHERE LIGHTS ARE DIM,
THAT PLACE I SEEK WHEN DAYS ARE GRIM.
TO TEND THOSE WOUNDS THAT NEVER HEAL,
THE DISTANT PAST THAT FEELS SO REAL.

A FUTILE GESTURE SOME WOULD SAY,
FOR THESE THINGS NEVER GO AWAY.
LIKE MONSTERS IN THE MURKY MIST,
REMINDING US THEY STILL EXIST.

THOUGH BATTLEWEARY, I REMAIN,
TOO MANY YEARS I'VE KNOWN THIS PAIN.
UNABLE STILL TO FREE MY HEART,
AS STILL MY PAST TEARS IT APART.

NOW THIS WAS NOT A PATH I CHOSE,
BUT SOMETIMES THAT'S JUST HOW IT GOES.
I'VE DONE MY BEST TO MAKE THINGS RIGHT,
BUT FOREVER I WILL FEAR THE NIGHT.

DELTA BLUE

KINDRED SPIRIT

ARE WE NOT ALL SPIRITS,
WITH KINDRED AS OUR NAME?
SHOULD WE NOT THEN ALL ENTWINE,
TO MAKE THAT SPECIAL FLAME?

TO FORM THAT PERFECT UNION,
THAT'S FOUND WHEN WE ARE ONE.
IT'S ONLY WHEN DIVIDED,
THAT WE CAN BE UNDONE.

YET UNITY ESCAPES US,
BUT THE BOOK STILL SAYS IT TRUE.
WHENEVER MAN IS OF ONE MIND,
THERES NOTHING HE CAN'T DO.

BUT I AM TOO AMBITIOUS,
IN WHAT I'D LIKE TO SEE.
TOO MUCH TO ASK, SUCH UNION,
OR SO IT SEEMS TO ME.

DELTA BLUE

BEHAVIORS

I DO NOT KNOW THE REASON,
WHY MAN DECIDES TO KILL.
IT MAKES AN EMPTINESS INSIDE,
A VOID WE CANNOT FILL.

THE CONSEQUENCES DIRE,
FOR BEHAVIOR SO EXTREME.
A PRODUCT OF OUR NATURE,
FOUND IN A NIGHTMARE DREAM.

BEYOND ALL HOPE OR REASON,
WE RETURN NOW TO THE FRAY.
IN AN ENDLESS EXECUTION,
OF THE SACRIFICIAL WAY.

THOUGH MAN THINKS HE'S STRONG NOW,
HIS WEAKNESS STILL SHINES CLEAR.
FOR HE WHO WILL NOT LEARN TO LOVE,
MUST LIVE A LIFE OF FEAR.

DELTA BLUE

BOOKENDS
(SONG)

NEVER DREAMED, I WOULD LEAVE YOU ALONE,
NEVER THOUGHT I'D SEE THE DAY,
BUT HERE I AM, WALKING OUT THE DOOR,
THOUGH THIS TIME I REALLY MEANT TO STAY.
WIND BLOWING, THROUGH YOUR HAIR;
WHEN I NEEDED, YOU WERE THERE.
ALL MY LIFETIME, OR SO IT SEEMS,
I'VE BEEN WALKING AWAY FROM MY DREAMS.

NOW PLEASE DON'T FORSAKE ME,
AND PLEASE DON'T MISTAKE ME.
DON'T KNOW WHAT MAKES ME
WALK ALONE.

WOMAN, I NEED YOU SO.
WOMAN, BUT I STILL HAVE TO GO.
WOMAN, OH YOU WERE SO RIGHT;
BUT I WAS BORN TO BE A RUNNER IN THE NIGHT.
WIND BLOWING, THROUGH YOUR HAIR,
WHEN I NEEDED, YOU WERE THERE.
ALL MY LIFETIME, OR SO IT SEEMS,
I'VE BEEN WALKING AWAY FROM MY DREAMS.

NOW PLEASE DON'T FORSAKE ME,
AND PLEASE DON'T MISTAKE ME.
DON'T KNOW WHAT MAKES ME
WALK ALONE.

DELTA BLUE

COMING DOWN HARD
(GOOD ACID—1973)

A SOUL IS THREATENED, LISTEN PLEASE;
I AM CRYING OUT IN FEAR.
AN UGLINESS HAS BREACHED MY WALLS;
THE SHADOWED PRINCE IS NEAR.

HIS POWER IS THE PRIDE OF MAN;
THE BLOOD HE PUMPS LIES COLD.
ENCRUSTED TO A LINE OF GREY,
THE ENDLESS LINES WHO SOLD.

AND AS THE SILENCE LINGERS ON;
CONFLICTING THOUGHTS SEEK RAGE.
AND I MUST HAVE THE STRENGTH TO TURN,
AND FIGHT THIS PRINCELY PAGE.

LAUGH LOUDLY FOOL, YOUR TIME IS LOST,
AND THE FUTURE'S HOPE LIES DIM.
DO NOT PLY YOUR CHILDISH IGNORANCE,
WITH YOUR BROTHERS PLIGHT SO GRIM.

FOR NOW A TIME IS DRAWING NEAR,
'TIS UNION COMRADES, LIGHT.
AT LAST THE FINAL CALL TO ARMS,
SOON THE BATTLE, DAY AND NIGHT.

FOR SUCH FORCES NOW DO GATHER,
THAT EXIST NOT ON THIS PLANE.
TO BE THROWN INTO THE BATTLE,
AND NONE SHALL REAP REMAINS.

NOT A STIRRING CRY OR MOVEMENT
WILL ESCAPE THE GROWING MOUND.
AS THE EVER SILENT MOUNTAINS
STAND AND GUARD THE BATTLEGROUND.

THUS IN MY MIND I STRUGGLE SO,
THROUGH TAINTED CLOUDS OF DEAD.
AS TWISTED LIMBS OF TIMES REMORSE,
NOW STAIN THE DAY WITH RED.

AND ALL ABOUT THE DAY RECEDES,
COMPELLED BY SATAN'S CALL.
FOR DARKNESS IS HIS KINGDOM,
AS HE WORKS TO DAMN US ALL.

DELTA BLUE

POLITICIANS

LIARS, LIARS, EVERYWHERE,
PICK YOUR PARTY, I DON'T CARE.
INNUENDOS, TACTICS LAME;
SEE THE CHILDREN PLAY THE GAME.

WHO'S THE LOSER? THEY ALL KNOW,
TALKING FAST AND WORKING SLOW.
EVERY YEAR THE SAME OLD LINE,
"VOTE FOR ME, AND YOU'LL BE FINE."

OH, CUT THE BULL, AND TELL IT STRAIGHT,
BEFORE WE FIND OUT IT'S TOO LATE.
CORRUPTED CONGRESS, HOUSE OF SHAME;
WHOSE TURN IS IT THIS TIME TO BLAME?

GO CHECK THE LATEST POLL TODAY,
SO YOU WILL KNOW JUST WHAT TO SAY.
BUT NEVER TELL US WHAT YOU FEEL;
I GUESS YOU CALL THAT BEING REAL.

I KNOW THAT THIS MAY SOUND EXTREME,
BUT SOMETIMES THAT'S JUST HOW IT SEEMS.
THE PRIVELEDGED CLASS, WITH SERFS STACKED DEEP,
WHO LOVE THE SHEARING OF THEIR SHEEP.

DELTA BLUE

THE CHILDREN

THEIR EYES ARE FRESH TO GREET THE DAY;
IT'S ALWAYS GOOD TO SEE THEM PLAY.
INSIDE THEIR HEARTS, HOPE STILL ABIDES,
BUT THAT'S WHAT COMES WITH BRAND NEW EYES.

YOU HEAR THEIR LAUGHTER ON THE WIND,
A JOYOUS SOUND THAT HAS NO END.
A LESSON TO BE LEARNED BY ALL,
THE MAGIC FOUND IN LAUGHTER'S CALL.

AND IN THEIR HEARTS WE ALL CAN FIND,
THE JOY OF LOVING UNCONFINED.
IT'S SAD THAT THERE WILL COME A DAY,
WHEN THE CHILD INSIDE US GOES AWAY.

YOU SEE THE WONDER IN THEIR FACE,
THIS WORLD IS STILL A BRAND NEW PLACE.
EACH DAY THEY ARE SO MUCH ALIVE;
I PRAY THEIR HOPES AND DREAMS SURVIVE.

DELTA BLUE

BOOT CAMP SONG
(SAN DIEGO-1967)

We're Mr. Field's troopers; we're fighters of the night.
We're dirty sons of bitches; we'd rather fuck than fight.
We'll castrate the Captain, with a dirty piece of glass,
And shove the broken Flagstaff up his ever-loving ass.

Oh singing, hidy tidy, Christ almighty, who the hell are we?
Zip, zap, jockey strap, it's Company 103.

I was walking down an alley, and much to my surprise;
I came upon an open door, and a girl with golden thighs.
She was wearing a pink kimono, that was open at the front,
And you could see the golden hairs around her golden cunt.
She took me by my hand then, and led me up those stairs,
And soon I found that very same hand, roaming through
those hairs.
And then I got the feeling, that feeling that's so grand;
I woke up in my Navy bunk with a discharge in my hand.

Oh singing, hidy tidy, Christ almighty, who the hell are we?
Zip, zap, jockey strap, it's Company 103.

May you have bloody hemorrhoids,
May corns adorn your feet.
May crabs as big as coconuts,
Sit on your balls and eat.
And when you're old and feeble,
An alcoholic wreck.

May your spine slip out your asshole,
And break your fucking neck.

Oh singing, hidy tidy, Christ almighty, who the hell are we?
Zip, zap, jockey strap, it's Company 103.

DELTA BLUE

CHILLICOTHE, TEXAS

I LOVED A GIRL, NOW GONE FROM ME.
I LOVE HER STILL, WHY SHOULD THIS BE?
HER FORM WAS SLIGHT, HER HAIR OF GOLD,
AND WHEN SHE SMILED, 'TWAS JOY UNTOLD.

I FOUND HER ON A WINTER'S MORN,
WHEN DAYS WERE COLD AND BLEAK.
AND I WAS WEARY OF THE NIGHT;
HER SHELTER I DID SEEK.

OUR LOVE WAS BRIEF, AND YET SO LONG.
THE YEARS THEY DID PASS BY.
AND THOUGH SHE IS NOW GONE FROM ME;
FOR HER I DO NOT CRY.

FOR SHE WAS ONE BORN FREE IN FLIGHT,
WITH WORLDS THAT SHE MUST FIND.
AND TO SEPARATE, WAS BEST FOR ALL;
TO SEPARATE WAS MOST KIND.

I'LL ALWAYS HAVE A PLACE FOR HER
DEEP DOWN INSIDE MY SOUL.
MY PRAYER IS THAT SHE FINDS HER WORLDS,
AND SOARS ABOVE HER GOALS.

TAKE CARE MY PRECIOUS LADY;
BE STRONG AND FLY SO HIGH.
MY WINGS WERE NOT AS STRONG AS YOURS;
'TWAS SAD I COULD NOT FLY.

BUT STANDING HERE AND WATCHING YOU
CLIMB UP THE LOFTY AIRS.
REMEMBER BACK DOWN HERE ON EARTH
IS ONE WHO REALLY CARES.

DELTA BLUE

INDIFFERENCE

NOW WE ALL KNEW THE PROBLEM,
BUT WE CHOSE NOT TO COMPLY.
PERHAPS WE WERE TOO BUSY NOW,
TO WATCH THE CHILDREN DIE.

YOU COULD SAY WE WERE CALLOUS,
SO INDIFFERENT TO THEIR NEEDS.
FOR WE ARE MORE IMPORTANT,
SO WE IGNORE THEIR PLEADS.

THEY SAY THAT WE'LL BE JUDGED NOW,
BY HOW WE TREAT THE LEAST.
BUT I HAVE THIS AWFUL FEELING,
WE'VE BEEN SIDING WITH THE BEAST.

THE POOR ARE WITH US ALWAYS,
THAT'S WHAT THE BOOK DOES SAY.
BUT TELL ME WHERE IT'S WRITTEN
THAT A CHILD CAN'T EAT TODAY.

I KNOW I'M SPEAKING FOOLISHLY,
IN A TIME WHEN WE SHOULD SHARE.
BUT THE NUMBERS AREN'T SUFFICIENT
FOR THIS WORLD TO REALLY CARE.

DELTA BLUE

PRIVELEGE

JUST TOOLS OF THEIR AMBITION,
THE LOFTY ONES WHO PLAY.
THE ENLIGHTENED ONES SO DISTANT
FROM THE PEOPLE THEY DISMAY.

THE CARTELS OF THE CALLUS,
THOSE ONES THEY CALL ELITE.
WHO DWELL INSIDE THEIR CASTLES,
WHILE THERE'S NOT ENOUGH TO EAT.

NO MATTER HOW THEY SHIMMER,
IN THEIR FINERY DISPLAYED.
PERCHED SAFELY IN THEIR TOWERS,
WHILE WE REMAIN DISMAYED.

THESE PRIVELEDGED ONES SO POMPOUS,
SO DISTANT NOW FROM NEED,
TO FAR ABOVE IT ALL NOW,
TO HEAR THE PEOPLES PLEAD.

THEY IGNORE THE CHILDREN'S HUNGER,
AMIDST CAVIAR AND CHAMPAGNE.
YES, MUCH TOO HIGH ABOVE IT ALL
TO KNOW THE PEOPLES PAIN.

DELTA BLUE

THE DOCTOR

THE DOC SAID HE HAD SEEN TOO MUCH,
THAT HE WAS SOMEHOW OUT OF TOUCH.
IT'S HARD TO EVER REALLY HEAL,
WHEN YOU ARE STILL AFRAID TO FEEL.

THE DOC SAID, "IT'S ALL IN HIS HEAD."
"PERHAPS HE'D SEEN TOO MANY DEAD."
HE TRIED TO TELL HIM WHAT HE'D SEEN,
ALTHOUGH THE SUBJECT WAS OBSCENE.

HE'D SOUGHT NOT HONOR, GLORY, FAME;
THOUGH ALL HE'D DONE SOME THOUGHT INSANE.
IT CAME NOT EASY TO HIS HEART,
TO TEAR SO MANY WORLDS APART.

THE DOC SAID, "IT'S ALL IN THE PAST."
"THIS NIGHTMARE NOW, IT WOULD NOT LAST."
BUT LOST INSIDE HIS WORLD TOO REAL,
HE WAS STILL AFRAID TO FEEL.

DELTA BLUE

THE WOODCARVER

HIS BLADE MOVED GENTLY, CARVING SLOW,
A JOYOUS ACT HE LOVED TO KNOW.
REMOVING PORTIONS NOT IN NEED,
IN SEARCH OF ALL HIS VISION'S PLEAD.

NOW BORN OF PASSIONS FOUND INSIDE,
FULFILLED CREATIONS UNDENIED.
HIS KNOWING HANDS DID GUIDE THE WOOD,
BETWEEN THEM BOTH IT'S UNDERSTOOD.

THE CAREFUL TOUCH, THE BLADE'S CARESS
THE WOOD RESPONDS TO TENDERNESS.
UNFOLDING NOW, A JOYOUS SIGHT,
REVEALING JUST WHAT HE THOUGHT RIGHT.

FREEING WHAT DID NOT BELONG,
TO LET THE WOOD NOW SING ITS SONG.
THE WOOD AND CARVER BOUND AS ONE,
IN A DANCE THAT'S NEVER DONE.

DELTA BLUE

THE LIGHT

OH, WE WERE REALLY SUCH A SIGHT.
A FLAMING STAR, SEEN IN THE NIGHT.
DURATION SHORT, BUT OH, SO BRIGHT,
YOU'VE HEARD ABOUT SUCH WONDEROUS LIGHT.

THE CREEPING DARKNESS STILL REMAINS,
BUT GRUDGINGLY, IT STILL ABSTAINS.
BEFORE THE RISING SUN'S DEMAND,
FOR IN THE LIGHT IS WHERE WE STAND.

DELTA BLUE

JINGLE BELLS

Jingle bells, mortar shells, V.C. in the grass.
We'll get no Merry Christmas, until this tour is passed.
Jingle bells, mortar shells, V.C. in the grass.
Take your homemade Christmas pies and shove them up
your ass.

Dashing through the mud, in a truck that should be junk.
O'er the roads we go, half of us are drunk.
Wheels on dirt roads bounce, making asses sore.
God I'd rather go to hell than finish out my tour.

Jingle bells, mortar shells, V.C. in the grass.
We'll get no Merry Christmas, until this tour is passed.
Jingle bells, mortar shells, V.C. in the grass.
Take your homemade Christmas pies and shove them up
your ass.

Christmas time is here, as everybody knows.
People think it's dear, G.I.'s think it blows.
All back home this day, watch the children play.
While we are getting shot at, every night, and every day.

Jingle bells, mortar shells, V.C. in the grass.
We'll get no Merry Christmas, until this tour is passed.
Jingle bells, mortar shells, V.C. in the grass.
Take your homemade Christmas pies and shove them up
your ass.

The moral to our song, is as plain as it can be.
No midnight carols sing, and fuck your Christmas tree.
There's one more thing to say, before we have to leave.
Vietnam is not the place to be on Christmas Eve.

Jingle bells, mortar shells, V.C. in the grass.
We'll get no Merry Christmas, until this tour is passed.
Jingle bells, mortar shells, V.C. in the grass.
Take your homemade Christmas pies and shove them up
your ass.

DELTA BLUE

JOSEPHINE
(FOR JOSEPHINE PATRICIA RUIZ—age 6)

A LITTLE ANGEL CAME TODAY,
TO BRIGHTEN UP OUR WORLD HER WAY.
A PRECIOUS WONDER, SHINING BRIGHT,
SOMEHOW SHE MAKES THE WORLD SEEM RIGHT.

THE HAPPY VISION ALWAYS SEEN,
THIS ANGEL WE CALL JOSEPHINE.
A SPARKLING JEWEL FROM UP ABOVE,
HE SENT TO US TO SHARE HIS LOVE.

FOR IN THE CHILD YOU FIND HIS HEART,
HE' S BEEN THERE FROM THE VERY START.
AND BRIGHTER NOW I'VE NEVER SEEN;
IT BURNS SO TRUE IN JOSEPHINE.

DELTA BLUE

WHISPERS ON THE WIND

WHISPERS ON THE WIND DECRY,
ALL THOSE THINGS WE DEIFY.
MOCKING NOW THE STRUCTURE TALL,
FOR WHAT CAN RISE CAN ALSO FALL.

NATIONS OFTEN NOW FORGET,
ONLY TO AGAIN REGRET.
AS FROM THE PAST THEY TOO DID RISE,
AND FALLING NOW, THEY FEIGN SURPRISE.

ONCE A NOBLE THOUGHT REIGNED FREE,
A SPIRIT SOME CALLED CHARITY.
FOR ALL OF US WHO HAD THE MIGHT,
MUST QUESTION NOW IF WE DID RIGHT.

THE WORLD IS SPINNING ROUND AND ROUND,
AND CHAOS IS OUR DAILY SOUND.
WITH PAIN AND HUNGER NEVER FAR,
FOR ALL OF US AN ANGRY SCAR.

I SEE THE CHILDREN AND I WEEP,
TOO MANY HELPLESS IN OUR KEEP.
WHAT WILL WE SAY TO GOD ON HIGH,
WHEN ASKED, "WHY DID WE LET THEM DIE?"

HE HAS TOLD US FROM THE START,
THE CHILDREN ALL LIVE IN HIS HEART.
A SACRED TRUST HE GAVE TO ALL,
I UNDERSTAND WHY WE WILL FALL.

DELTA BLUE

LOVE

WHEN I LOOKED INTO HER EYES,
IT HIT ME, AND I REALIZED.
THAT IN MY HEART WHERE LOVE CAN GROW
IT WAS A LOVE I'D NEVER KNOW.

FOR SHE HAD FOUND THE ONE SHE SOUGHT,
THOUGH SHE WAS WRONG, IT MATTERED NOT.
AND THOUGH HE NEVER WOULD BE TRUE,
THERE WAS NOTHING, I COULD DO.

I WATCHED IN SILENCE, AS SHE CRIED;
HE HAD NO LOVE FOR HER INSIDE.
HIS WORDS HAD CUT HER, 'TILL SHE BLED.
HER LIFE WENT ON, BUT SHE WAS DEAD.

THERE ISN'T MUCH THAT YOU CAN DO
WHEN SOMEONE LOVES ANOTHER TRUE.
I KNEW THAT SOMEWHERE DEEP INSIDE,
THE MAGIC IN HER HEART HAD DIED.

NO MORE WAS WONDER IN HER EYE,
HER LAUGHTER HAD BECOME A LIE.
THERE IS A TRUTH, NOW, OH SO REAL.
IT'S ONLY WHEN YOU LOVE, YOU HEAL.

DELTA BLUE

MY LADY
(LYRICS)

BEEN TOO FAR AND I CARRY THE SCAR
OF A WAR THAT I DIDN'T CHOOSE.
I FOUND NO THRILL WHEN I HAD TO KILL;
TOO MANY BROTHERS NOW PAID THEIR DUES.
SO I CAME HOME AND I FELT SO ALONE,
THAT DEPRESSION WAS MY FRIEND.
THEN I FOUND YOU AND LIFE BECAME NEW,
AND ALL MY SCARS BEGAN TO MEND.

OH, MY LADY, I COULD NEVER SAY
HOW MUCH YOU HEALED ME,
CHASED THE DARKNESS FROM MY DAY.
SO MUCH EVIL, UGLINESS I KNEW,
NO LONGER HAUNTS ME,
AND IT'S ALL BECAUSE OF YOU.

WAR IS HELL AND I COULDN'T TELL
OF SO MANY THINGS I'VE DONE.
I FEEL THE FEAR OF DEATH, OH SO NEAR,
LOSING BROTHERS WAS NEVER FUN.
SOMETIMES THAT FRIGHT WILL RETURN IN THE
NIGHT,
AND I'LL AWAKEN WITH A SCREAM.
TOO MANY YEARS TO LIVE WITH THE FEARS,
EVEN THOUGH THEY'RE ONLY DREAMS.

OH MY LADY, YOU WERE SO VERY KIND,
GAVE ME THE STRENGTH TO SEE.
WHEN I WAS LOST AND BLIND,
SO MUCH EVIL, UGLINESS I KNEW
NO LONGER HAUNTS ME,
AND IT'S ALL BECAUSE OF YOU.

DELTA BLUE

HOT RAILS TO HELL

GONNA TAKE YOU HIGHER,
UP INTO THE SKY.
GONNA BRING YOU FIRE,
KNOW THE REASON WHY.
FEEL IT CALLING OUT TO YOU
THOSE MAGIC GLEAMING ROWS,
THAT LIE AND STARE, AND SOMEHOW DARE
THEN VANISH UP YOUR NOSE.

OH, THOSE HOT RAILS, RIDING HOT RAILS TO HELL.
YOU CAN RIDE OR PASS ON BY,
BUT THOSE HOT RAILS ARE BURNING IN MY SOUL;
GOT TO RIDE, GOT TO FLY.

OH, IT BRINGS YOU THE THUNDER,
AND THEN IT LETS YOU KNOW
THAT DEEP INSIDE IS THE POWER,
SO ALIVE, FEEL IT GROW.
THEN COMES THE LIGHTNING;
SET FREE, SO DEEP INSIDE.
JUST TAKE THE TIME TO WONDER.
OH, HOW I LOVE TO RIDE.

OH THOSE HOT RAILS, CAN YOU HEAR THAT SOUND?
OH, THOSE HOT RAILS, COMING ON THRU.
RIDING HOT RAILS, I'M TAKING THE HIGH ROAD
'TILL I BREAK ON THROUGH.

IT'S A ROAD FULL OF VALLEYS,
AND MOUNTAIN PEAKS SO HIGH.
BUFFED UP LINES TO FREE THE MINDS,
OF THOSE WHO CAME TO FLY.

IT'S A FREEWAY OF HARD TIMES,
AND A MISTRESS SO COLD.
BUT WHEN YOU'RE TALL, AND DOING IT ALL,
IT'S SO FINE BEING BOLD.

HEY THERE BUDDY,
HAVE YOU EVER BEEN RIDING?
DID YOU WONDER ABOUT THAT ROAD?
MAKING A DRIVE, TRYING TO STAY ALIVE,
HOT RAILS TO EASE MY LOAD.

DELTA BLUE

THE WALK

GOD LOOKED DOWN
ON THIS CHILD AND SAID,
"IF YOU WALK THAT PATH,"
"YOU'LL SOON BE DEAD."
THE BOY LOOKED SLOWLY TO THE SKY,
SAID, "DON'T YOU TELL ME HOW TO DIE."

I KNOW THE PRICE,
I'LL PAY THE TOLL.
YOU KNOW MY HEART,
YOU KNOW MY SOUL.
AND IF INDEED I FALL THIS DAY,
KNOW IN YOUR HEART I WALKED MY WAY.

FOR WHEN I FADE INTO THAT NIGHT,
MY PRAYER IS THAT I DID IT RIGHT.
AND THOUGH THE DARKNESS KNOWS MY NAME,
IT IS NOT MY GOD'S DOMAIN.
IN WAR OR PEACE I'LL WALK HIS WAY,
"BUT IT MUST BE MY PATH," I SAY.

DELTA BLUE

BULLDOZER

(SONG)

WELL, I'VE BEEN WORKING
JUST LIKE A DOG.
EVERYDAY IS WALKING
THROUGH A BLINDING FOG.
THERE ARE PEOPLE AROUND ME
WHO TRY TO PULL ME DOWN.
THEY WANT TO STOP ME,
BUT I CAN'T BE FOUND.
HERE COMES THE POWER,
ROLLING OVER THE PLAIN.
THIS BOY AIN'T EVER
GETTING OFF OF THIS TRAIN.

THEY KEEP PUTTING WALLS IN FRONT OF ME,
AND I KEEP TEARING THEM DOWN.
IT'S MY TIME TO GO WALKING NOW,
THEIR TURN TO GO AROUND.
WITH ANGER NOW MY DAILY SOUND,
FROM THOSE WHO NOW DEMAND THEIR POUND.

MOVING DOWN THAT HIGHWAY,
MOVING DOWN THAT LINE.
GONNA DO IT MY WAY;
GETTING BY AND FEELING FINE.
AND LIVE THE ONE THING I HAVE LEARNED,
THAT MAKES A BRIGHTER DAY.
ALWAYS LISTEN TO YOUR HEART,
AND WHAT IT HAS TO SAY.

DELTA BLUE

TRUCKIN'
(LYRICS)

RUNNING FREE, THRU THE STREETS OF THE CITY.
FEEL THE WIND ON MY SKIN AS I RIDE.
HEAR IT CALL, FROM THE ROAD TO MY SOUL NOW.
WASHING OVER ME, JUST LIKE THE TIDE.

WHEN MY SOUL'S OUT OF CONTROL SHE WILL CALL ME.
"COME TO ME, AND BE FREE ON MY ROAD".
AS THE PAIN SLIPS AWAY, LET THE MILES HAVE THEIR SAY.
DRIFT AWAY, DRIFT AWAY, LOSE THE LOAD.

BEEN A RUNNER, TOO LONG IN THIS LIFETIME.
BATTLES FOUGHT IN THE PAST TAUGHT ME WELL.
ROLLING MILES, EASING TRIALS, ENDLESS HIGHWAY.
RIDE AWAY, RIDE AWAY, TIME WILL TELL.

FROM THE NIGHT, TOWARD THE LIGHT, AND THE DAWNING,
AS THE ROAD CARRIES ME, WAY BACK HOME.
MAYBE TIME, AND ITS RHYME, THEY WILL FIND ME,
AND NO LONGER WILL THIS CHILD EVER ROAM.

DELTA BLUE

SOLUTIONS

THERE ARE CERTAINLY SOLUTIONS,
THAT ARE FOUND NOW WITH A FIST.
AND INDEED THERE ARE THOSE PEOPLE,
WE ALL KNOW WHO INSIST.

NOW A CERTAIN SATISFACTION,
CAN BE FOUND NOW IN THE TASK,
OF GIVING TO THAT PERSON
EXACTLY WHAT THEY ASKED.

DON'T ASK ME WHY THEY WANT THIS,
FOR I DO NOT UNDERSTAND.
BUT REARRANGING CARTILAGE
IS NOT MUCH OF A PLAN

NOW SOME WOULD CALL ME SHAMELESS,
FOR DOING WHAT THEY ASK.
BUT JUST A BIT, I MUST ADMIT,
SOMETIMES I LOVE THE TASK.

DELTA BLUE

PLACES

I GUARD A PLACE THAT LIVES IN ME,
WHERE I CAN GO AND YOU CAN'T SEE.
THOSE TIMES WHEN I CAN'T CARRY ON,
THOSE TIMES WHEN I'M NO LONGER STRONG.

A PLACE INSIDE WHERE LIGHTS ARE DIM,
THAT PLACE I SEEK WHEN DAYS ARE GRIM.
TO TEND THOSE WOUNDS THAT NEVER HEAL,
THE DISTANT PAST THAT FEELS SO REAL.

A FUTILE GESTURE SOME WOULD SAY,
FOR THESE THINGS NEVER GO AWAY.
LIKE MONSTERS IN THE MURKY MIST,
REMINDING US THEY STILL EXIST.

THOUGH BATTLEWEARY, I REMAIN,
TOO MANY YEARS I'VE KNOWN THIS PAIN.
UNABLE STILL TO FREE MY HEART,
AS STILL MY PAST TEARS IT APART.

NOW THIS WAS NOT A PATH I CHOSE,
BUT SOMETIMES THAT'S JUST HOW IT GOES.
I'VE DONE MY BEST TO MAKE THINGS RIGHT,
BUT FOREVER I WILL FEAR THE NIGHT.

DELTA BLUE

MY CAR

MY CAR KNOWS I HAVE MONEY,
MY CAR KNOWS I CAN PAY.
MY CAR KNOWS THERE'S A SURPLUS,
MY CAR IS MEAN THAT WAY.

DON'T TELL ME THEY AREN'T PSYCHIC;
DON'T TELL ME THEY DON'T SEE.
MY CAR KNOWS HOW MUCH I WILL GET,
BEFORE IT GETS TO ME.

MY CAR THINKS THIS IS FUNNY;
MY CAR WILL MAKE ME PAY.
MY CAR KNOWS I'VE A TAX REFUND,
SO ITS TRANNY WENT AWAY.

OH, MUCH TOO LIKE A WOMAN,
MY CAR AND MONEY NOW.
NO MATTER HOW MUCH THAT I MAKE,
IT NEEDS IT ALL SOMEHOW

DELTA BLUE

NAMES

LONG WINDED AND MISGUIDED,
ARE MONIKERS THAT FIT.
BUT THERE ARE THOSE WHO'LL TELL YOU
THEY THINK I'M FULL OF SHIT.

NOW I DON'T REALLY MIND THAT;
IT'S STICKS AND STONES TO ME.
I DON'T PRETEND TO BE RIGHT;
IT'S JUST THE WAY I SEE.

STILL THOSE WHO DISAGREE NOW
WITH VIEWS THAT I ESPOUSE.
SAY THAT MY METHANE OUTPUT
EXCEEDS THAT OF THE COWS.

BUT THAT DOES NOT DISTURB ME;
I LET THEIR COMMENTS PASS.
'CAUSE ALL THEY'RE REALLY SAYING IS
I'M JUST A NATURAL GAS.

DELTA BLUE

THE GUITAR MAN

FAR OFF IN THE DISTANCE,
WALKS THE MUSIC MAN.
ON HIS SHOULDERS, A BATTERED GUITAR,
JUST LOOKING FOR A PLACE TO MAKE A STAND.

ON HIS FACE ARE THE HARSH LINES,
OF ALL THE DUES HE'S PAID.
BUT HIS EYES STILL HOLD THE WONDER,
OF THE MUSIC THAT HE HAS MADE.

PLAY A SONG, MR. GUITAR MAN,
PLAY A SONG FOR ME.
PLAY IT LONG, AND PLAY IT STRONG,
'CAUSE THAT'S HOW IT MUST BE.

SAIL AWAY GUITAR MAN,
UP INTO THE SKY.
TAKE ME TOO, MR. GUITAR MAN.
HELP ME FLY, HELP ME FLY.

THEN HE TURNED IN SILENCE,
AND WALKED INTO THE DAWN.
BEFORE WE EVER KNEW IT,
THE GUITAR MAN WAS GONE.

WHAT DID HE TRY TO TELL US?
WHAT DID HE TRY TO SAY?
THAT ALL ALONG, YOU SHOULD SING YOUR SONG,
AND LIVE IT DAY BY DAY.

DELTA BLUE

DIATRIBE

YOU KNOW THAT YOU CAN'T DO IT,
"IMPOSSIBLE," HE SAID.
YOUR FATE IS SEALED REGARDLESS,
JUST FACE THE FACTS INSTEAD.

DON'T TELL ME WHAT I CAN'T DO,
WHAT'S POSSIBLE MY WAY.
FOR I KNOW YOU ARE WRONG NOW;
I'M LIVING PROOF EACH DAY.

IT'S JUST ANOTHER BATTLE,
IT'S JUST ANOTHER TEST.
IT'S JUST ANOTHER ACTION,
TAKEN IN THE LIFELONG QUEST.

TOMORROW'S JUST A PROMISE,
YOU HOPE THAT GOD WILL KEEP.
SO YOU CAN KNOW THE SHELTER,
OF HIS ARMS NOW AS YOU SLEEP.

DELTA BLUE

SILLY STUFF

SHE SAID SHE DIDN'T EAT MEAT,
IT'S SO VULGAR NOW TO KILL.
JUST THE THOUGHT OF EATING FLESH,
WAS ENOUGH TO MAKE HER ILL.

SHE TALKED ABOUT THEIR PAIN NOW,
HOW BRUTAL THEIR DEMISE.
I SAID I UNDERSTOOD NOW,
AS I ATE MY CHICKEN THIGHS.

I STOPPED HER WITH A GESTURE,
SAID, "I MEANT NOT TO OFFEND."
HAD SHE NOTICED RICE LAMENTING
AS THEY CONTEMPLATED THEIR END?

DID SHE HEAR THE BEANS ALL PRAYING?
JUST BEFORE THEIR SALTY BOIL.
OR ASPARAGUS BEING BURNED ALIVE,
IN SEARING OLIVE OIL?

SHE SAID THAT FISH WERE MEATLESS.
WELL, YOU LOOK THEM IN THE EYE,
AND TELL THEM THEY ARE VEGGIES;
THAT'S WHY THEY GET TO DIE.

I'VE HEARD THE LETTUCE SCREAMING,
IN THE SALAD SHOOTER'S BLADES.
I'M HAUNTED BY THOSE CABBAGES,
AS THEY DROWNED IN HOLLANDAISE.

I REMEMBER BROCCOLI BEGGING,
AS YOUR TEETH TORE THEM APART.
SO STOP IT WITH THE VEGGIES,
ALL THEY DO IS MAKE ME FART.

DELTA BLUE

"THE FECAL MATTER"
(DEDICATED TO ALL MY FELLOW BURNERS)

THE JOB WAS GRIM, I TELL YOU,
A THANKLESS TASK AT BEST.
IT HAD A SPECIAL "AIR" THOUGH,
TO THAT I CAN ATTEST.

I APPROACHED THIS JOB WITH CAUTION,
EIGHT DRUMS WERE MY DOMAIN.
A TASK REQUIRED OFTEN,
WITH THE DIESEL AND THE FLAME.

AMAZING THE PRODUCTION,
AND THE QUANTITY THAT FLOWED.
THE WAY THEY FILLED THOSE DRUMS UP,
A FECES OVERLOAD.

THE DAY THAT CHARLIE FOUND IT,
WITHOUT IT, WE FELT LOST.
A MORTAR NOW, RIGHT ON THE NOSE,
A "FECES" HOLOCAUST.

ONE HIT AND IT WAS GONE NOW,
A LOSS OF DEEP REGRET.
THERE WAS SO MUCH FECES EVERYWHERE,
YOU'D THINK THAT CONGRESS MET.

DELTA BLUE

HOW SWEET THE LIGHT

SOFTLY SHARING,
PASSIONS FLOW,
INTO THAT LAND
WHERE LOVE CAN GROW.

HARSH THE WORLD,
NOW SHIELDED STRONG,
BY TWO HEARTS
THAT NOW BELONG.

SAD THE SOUL,
THAT CANNOT DARE.
FOR WE ARE NOTHING,
'TILL WE CARE.

SEE THEIR SPIRIT
MOCK THE SUN.
HOW SWEET THE LIGHT,
WHEN TWO ARE ONE.

DELTA BLUE

BREAK THE CHAIN

THE WIND COMES SOFTLY TO MY SOUL;
SHE SHOWS ME HER NIGHT SKY.
AND SOFTLY HEARD THE VOICES SPEAK,
THOSE TRUTHS NONE CAN DENY.

WE ARE PRISONERS OF THE PAST;
A DUTY, HONOR BOUND.
FOR WE ARE KEEPERS OF THEIR FLAME;
YES, THOSE ON HALLOWED GROUND.

OUR DUTY IS TO CARRY ON,
TO STAND THE LINE EACH DAY.
AND LIVE A LIFE DEEMED WORTHY,
BY THOSE WHO COULD NOT STAY.

FOR FUTURE GENERATIONS,
MUST HEAR ABOUT OUR PAIN.
PERHAPS THEY'LL LEARN AND SOMEDAY BE,
THE ONES WHO BREAK THE CHAIN.

DELTA BLUE

THE LAST MISSION

For Sgt. R. M. Gomez 2/177th 1st Infantry Div.
In Memory of Cpl. Hipolito "Johnny" Camargo
1/198th Americal Div.

ONE LAST PATROL WAS WAITING,
ONE MISSION LEFT UNDONE.
JUST ONE FINAL DUTY,
TELL A MOTHER, ABOUT HER SON.

THAT DAY WAS ALWAYS LOOMING,
AND IT HAD COME AT LAST.
HE MADE THE FINAL JOURNEY,
RETURNED NOW TO THE PAST

HE LOOKED THEM IN THE EYE THERE,
AND SAID WHAT MUST BE SAID.
HOW IN THE BATTLE'S FURY,
IT WAS THEIR SON WHO LED.

IT POURED OUT OF HIS HEART NOW,
HE TOLD THE STORY TRUE.
ABOUT THAT DAY HIS BEST FRIEND DIED,
WITH NOTHING HE COULD DO.

HE REACHED THE PAINFUL ENDING,
A PROMISE FINALLY KEPT.
TOO LONG THE OPEN WOUND NOW,
OF WHY THEIR SON NOW SLEPT.

AND IN THE FINAL SHARING,
A BOND OF LOVE REMAINED.
THEY WERE FOREVER BROTHERS,
THAT'S HOW IT WAS ORDAINED.

DELTA BLUE

REQUIEM

THE SILENT ONE THEY CALLED HIM,
SOMEONE THAT'S NEVER KNOWN.
THE LOOK UPON HIS FACE NOW,
SAID JUST LEAVE HIM ALONE.

A WANDERER, A NOMAD,
COMPELLED TO ALWAYS ROAM.
UNCAGED, A TIGER, DRIVEN MAD,
ADRIFT WITHOUT A HOME.

HE WAS A SCAR OF BATTLE,
HIS GUN HAD SCREAMED HIS PAIN.
HE'D ASKED GOD TO FORGIVE HIM,
FOR HE WAS LOST AGAIN.

A DANGER TO ENCOUNTER,
WITH ALL HIS TROUBLED WAYS.
CONSUMED BEYOND HIS REASON,
BY THE DARKNESS OF HIS DAYS.

HE SOUGHT NO FURTHER STRUGGLE,
NO CONFLICT TO ENGAGE.
HE'D JUST BEEN PUSHED TOO FAR TOO FAST;
HE COULD NOT TURN THE PAGE.

HIS HEART HE KEPT WELL-GUARDED,
HIS SECURITY SEVERE.
HE'D NEVER LET ANOTHER KNOW,
ABOUT HIS WORLD OF FEAR.

HOW COULD HE EVER TELL THEM?
WHAT LIVED INSIDE HIS SOUL.
WHY WOULD HE EVER WANT THEM?
TO KNOW HE LOST CONTROL.

FOREVER CLAD IN ARMOR,
A LOWERED SHIELD NO MORE.
DEFIANT TO HIS ENDING NOW,
AS HE HELD OFF THE WAR.

THERE WAS ONE THING ABOUT HIM,
THAT WAS NO IDLE BOAST.
HE WAS THE SUM OF ALL HIS FEARS,
AND HE FEARED HIMSELF THE MOST.

DELTA BLUE

FARE THEE WELL

I THINK THIS DAY IS PROPER
I THINK THIS DAY WILL DO
FOR NOW THE TIME IS GROWING NEAR
TO SAY FAREWELL TO YOU

IT'S JUST THE WAY THINGS WORK OUT.
IT'S JUST THE WAY THINGS ARE.
WHAT'S LEFT NOW IN MY JOURNEY,
IS NOT THAT VERY FAR.

I HOPE I BROUGHT YOU LAUGHTER
I KNOW I MADE YOU SAD
BUT THAT WAS JUST MY NATURE
TO NOT LEAVE OUT THE BAD

FOREVER IN MY HEART NOW
YOU HAVE FOUND A PLACE
ETERNAL IN MY SOUL NOW
AS I SEEK NOW HIS GRACE

DO NOT CRY FOR ME MY FRIEND
NO SHED YOU NOT A TEAR
FOR I GO TO A BETTER PLACE
A LAND I KNOW IS NEAR

NO FURTHER COMMENT NEEDED
I TURN AND GO MY WAY
AND LEAVE THE COMMENTARY
FOR SOMEONE ELSE TO SAY

DELTA BLUE

PENANCE

IN HIS HEART, STILL LIVED THE SHAME
OF ALL THE WRONG HE'D BEEN
ANOTHER WAYWARD CHILD OF GOD
ALL COVERED UP IN SIN

A WITNESS TO THE DARKNESS
FOUND IN THE SOUL OF MAN
SURVIVOR OF THE MADNESS
THAT NO ONE UNDERSTANDS

A BENDED KNEE SUBMISSION
TO THE ONLY ONE STILL REAL
SURRENDERS NOW THIS SOLDIER
WHO'S HAD TOO MUCH TO FEEL

UNRECONCILED THIS TORMENT
HE BROUGHT BEFORE HIS KING
FOR ONLY HIS FORGIVENESS NOW
COULD EVER WASH HIM CLEAN

DELTA BLUE

Printed in the United States
93717LV00008B/67-69/A